2835 1822   7/02

W9-BFZ-450

WITHDRAWN
BEAVERTON CITY LIBRARY
Beaverton, OR 97005
Member of Washington County
COOPERATIVE LIBRARY SERVICES

IN THIS SERIES

Auto Racing

Baseball

Basketball

Bodybuilding

Extreme Sports

Field Hockey

Figure Skating

Football

Golf

Gymnastics

Hockey

Lacrosse

Martial Arts

Soccer

Softball

Strongman Competition

Tennis

Track and Field

Volleyball

Wrestling

THE COMPOSITE GUIDE

to GYMNASTICS

RICHARD HUFF

CHELSEA HOUSE PUBLISHERS

Philadelphia

Produced by Choptank Syndicate, Inc. and Chestnut Productions

Senior Editor: Norman L. Macht
Editor and Picture Researcher: Mary E. Hull
Design and Production: Lisa Hochstein
Cover Illustrator: Cliff Spohn

Project Editor: Jim McAvoy
Art Direction: Sara Davis
Cover Design: Keith Trego

© 2000 by Chelsea House Publishers,
a subsidiary of Haights Cross Communications.
Printed and bound in the United States of America.

First Printing

1 3 5 7 9 8 6 4 2

Library of Congress Cataloging-in-Publication Data

Huff, Richard M.
     The composite guide to gymnastics / by Richard Huff.
          p.   cm.— (The composite guide)
     Includes bibliographical references (p. 62) and index.
     Summary: Discusses the history of gymnastics and the development of different
gymnastic events that are part of Olympic competition.
     ISBN 0-7910-5865-4
     1. Gymnastics—History—Juvenile literature. 2. Olympics—History—Juvenile literature.
[1. Gymnastics—History. 2. Olympics] I. Title: Gymnastics. II. Title. III. Series.
GV461.3 .H84 2000
796.44—dc21
                                                          00-020728

CONTENTS

CHAPTER 1
One Jump Away from the Gold 7

CHAPTER 2
Naked Exercise 15

CHAPTER 3
All About the Competition 23

CHAPTER 4
Women Lead the Way 33

CHAPTER 5
America Brings Home the Gold 41

CHAPTER 6
The Current and Future Stars 53

Chronology 59

Glossary 61

Further Reading 62

Index 63

ONE JUMP AWAY FROM THE GOLD

The United States women's Olympic gymnastics team, some of whom were as young as 14, woke up on the morning of July 24, 1996, with the strongest chance the country had ever had of winning a women's team gold medal.

The team, a group of athletes including such veteran gymnasts as Shannon Miller, Dominique Dawes, Kerri Strug, Amy Chow, Amy Borden, Jaycie Phelps, and a new star, 14-year-old Dominique Moceanu, started the day second to the Russians, who held a slim lead after the first round of compulsory exercises.

For years, European teams dominated the team competition in gymnastics, specifically women's gymnastics. In 1972 a young gymnast named Olga Korbut won three gold medals at the summer Olympics in Munich, leading her Soviet team to a championship and wowing the world. The same country won the team medal four years later.

But now, 20 years later, the focus would be on a new group of young women from the United States. The setting for the event was Atlanta, Georgia, which in some ways gave the U.S. team a home-court advantage.

By being in the states, more of their families could attend than if the Olympics were held abroad. They would not have to adapt to the cultural changes faced by athletes when competing

Despite an injury, Kerri Strug managed to nail the landing on her second vault and earned a score that secured the first-ever team gold medal for the U.S. women at the 1996 Olympics in Atlanta, Georgia.

Members of the United States women's gymnastics team wave to the crowd after being awarded their gold medals in the team competition at the 1996 summer Olympics. From left to right are Amanda Borden, Dominique Dawes, Amy Chow, Jaycie Phelps, Dominique Moceanu, Kerri Strug, and Shannon Miller.

in a foreign country. Everything has an impact on an athlete.

The team worked smoothly throughout the first three of four events that comprised the optional portion of the competition.

Gymnastic judges use a subjective ratings system based on a 10-point total. In the judging of optional events in women's gymnastics, difficulty accounts for five points, originality and composition for two, execution and amplitude for two, and general impression for one point. Errors result in deductions; the sport uses a precise points system for each mistake.

Points are awarded based on the judges' impressions of a gymnast's performance on any given day. So, though rare, a perfect score of 10 doesn't necessarily mean there is no room for improvement in a gymnast's work.

Early in the day, the U.S. gymnasts performed flawlessly in the parallel bars, an exercise using two bars of similar height and length, with Miller, Strug, and Phelps each scoring 9.787. Dawes and Moceanu each earned 9.8.

Then Miller and Moceanu recorded a 9.8623 and a 9.85 respectively for their performances on the balance beam, which were executed while standing atop a long beam, just several inches wide. A good balance beam performance looks like it's being done on the floor.

Later, Moceanu earned a 9.837 with her floor exercise, which she performed to the sounds of Charlie Daniels's country hit, "The Devil Went Down to Georgia." Dawes also earned a 9.85 in the floor exercises.

Generally speaking, the U.S. women's gymnastics team made it all look easy on this hot July day. There were no major slipups, no falls, and nothing to look back on and wish they had done better. They held a large .897-point lead over the Russians. Barring a major disaster, they were on their way to an Olympic gold medal, one that had eluded the U.S. since the women's team competition was created for the 1928 Olympics.

Between 1952 and 1976, the award had gone seven times to Russian teams, and now, on a summer night in Georgia, the American women were on the verge of taking home the coveted gold medal, the international symbol for sporting excellence.

What stood between them and the gold was the vaulting competition, in which each participant races down a short runway at full speed, jumps off a small springboard, and performs an athletic feat in midair. The vaulting competition stems from an artificial horse originally used by knights. The horse is a heavily padded device, 5' wide and standing just over 3' 6" tall. It's a mere 16 inches across the top.

Vaulting may require the greatest amount of strength of any women's gymnastic event. It takes a matter of seconds to complete. Yet the performance is strenuous and physical. After hurling her body into the air, a gymnast must execute a series of moves before positioning herself for a safe landing.

Going into the vaulting competition, the final event for the women, the U.S. team was again on a roll. Four of the members hit perfect vaults, leaving Moceanu and Strug to finish off the Russians, who had already stumbled and trailed the U.S. Then disaster struck. Moceanu fell twice on her vaults. She slipped backwards on both landings. Her score was a 9.200.

Under gymnastic rules, Moceanu's score could be tossed out if Strug, who had yet to jump, could do better. As it stood at that moment, the Russians had a statistical chance to spoil the U.S. team's shot at the gold.

Strug, a sprightly 88-pound gymnast, had been vaulting for a decade. Her coach was Bela Karolyi, the man who helped make Nadia Comaneci one of the greatest gymnasts in the history of the sport. He had coached gold

medalist Mary Lou Retton and was also over-seeing the work of Moceanu.

Strug, the pressure of winning a team gold medal on her shoulders, launched her tiny body toward the vault. When she landed, her feet slipped out from underneath her. She fell backward, landing on her bottom. The judges posted a dismal 9.16 for the jump, one of the worst scores by an American gymnast that day. But, besides the score, Strug was hurt. Later she learned she had torn two ligaments in her ankle.

U.S.A.'s Kerri Strug is carried by her coach, Bela Karolyi, on her way to receiving her gold medal for the women's team gymnastics competition at the 1996 summer Olympics in Atlanta. Strug tore two ligaments and sprained her ankle during the vault competition.

"After the first vault, I heard a snap in my foot," Strug said later. "It hurt a lot."

But, perhaps, not as much as the potential of losing the medal, which was so close.

"I can't feel my leg," Strug told her coach before a hushed crowd of more than 32,000 people.

"Shake it out, shake it out," Karolyi, a tough taskmaster told her. "Give me one last good vault."

At the time, Karolyi was convinced the Russians had a chance of surpassing the U.S. for the top spot. So he pushed Strug to return to the starting line. She hobbled into position, her face tense with pain and emotion.

"I knew that the gold was kind of slipping away," Strug said. "I said a little prayer, 'Please God, help me out here. I've done this thousands of times . . . just one more.'"

She waited for the green light that indicated it was time to run. And she ran. She cartwheeled onto the springboard and flew backwards off the vault. She planted her feet on the landing, grimacing in pain as she waited for enough time to pass. Once she had stood for the regulated amount of time, Strug fell to the floor.

The judges posted a 9.712 score for Strug, and the U.S. won the gold.

"If it was me, I'd have gone out there on a broken leg," Karolyi said afterward. "This was history. This was a once-in-a-lifetime situation."

Strug was carried out of the arena on a stretcher a few minutes later, begging to be allowed to remain at the venue until after the medal ceremony, which would follow. She emerged from the locker room minutes later in the arms of Karolyi, her badly injured leg wrapped in bandages. When it was over, Karolyi carried her back to the stretcher for a ride to the hospital.

"The U.S. is no longer a follower in the world of gymnastics," Olympic commentator Mary Lou Retton said then. "After so many generations, the U.S. is a leader. This is history."

2

NAKED EXERCISE

The sport of gymnastics, or at least some form of it, has been around for more than 2,000 years. Of course, back then it was not as organized or as flashy as it is today.

The earliest mentions of gymnastics date back to ancient Egypt and are credited to acrobats. But even earlier, men and women of the Minoan culture on the island of Crete participated in bull leaping, an athletic event that may have actually been the forerunner of today's vault competition.

In bull leaping, a participant would run toward a charging bull, grab its horns, and while being thrown upward, complete a variety of maneuvers, before landing on the bull's back. Provided all went well, the performer would then dismount from the back of the bull. Bull leaping was a tremendously dangerous feat. While the men were certainly daring, it's believed they didn't go into the competition without at least a minimal amount of training. Before the men actually performed their stunts on real animals, they practiced on an apparatus which has been likened to an early form of the pommel horse used in competition today.

The word gymnastics is derived from the Greek "gymnos," meaning naked. Gymnastics means naked exercise. Athletes in Greece worked on their skills at schools for naked exercise, which were limited to male participants.

Women gymnasts work out at a gym ca. 1920. In 1928, women's gymnastics became an official Olympic sport.

Gymnastics is now a broad term used to describe a series of physical exercises designed for therapeutic or educational purposes. Today some of those exercises are still used to help relieve discomfort suffered by disabled people. Educational gymnastics is a program that challenges students to complete a series of moves that involve strength, flexibility, and conditioning.

The current form of indoor gymnastics has its roots in Greece, where three forms of gymnastic exercises were developed. One form was designed to develop excellent physical conditions; another was used to train the military; a third was created to condition athletes for other sports, such as wrestling or running.

To the Greeks, the ideal was to train the mind and the body. A man who neglected his body was considered an incomplete person.

The teachers of those programs in Greece were the first to offer them to both the military and the public. At the time, the teaching of gymnastic regimens was considered a key part of a child's education. Greeks believed that the "unity" of a child's mind and body could only happen through participation in exercise.

The Romans also used gymnastics to develop strength. But after the fall of the Western Roman Empire, in the fourth and fifth centuries, the concept of exercise fell by the wayside. From the Middle Ages to the Renaissance, the most popular form of physical activity was jousting among knights.

The form of gymnastics known today started to take hold in Germany in the 1800s. Friendrich Ludwig Jahn, a German high school teacher, has been called the "father of

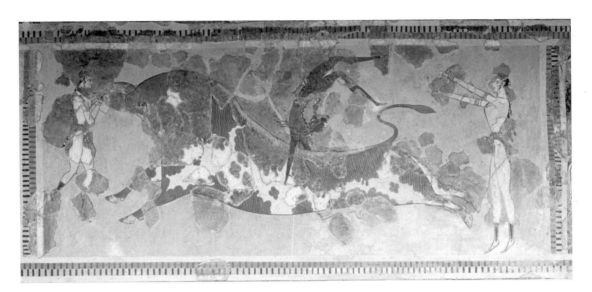

gymnastics," having developed a group of exercises using stationary apparatus to meet essentially the same goals of self-discipline and strength set up by the Greeks centuries earlier.

Besides teaching gymnastics, Jahn also used his gym, then called Turnvereins, to offer commentary on the political situation throughout Europe at the time. Jahn's regimen of gymnastics, combined with talk of intellectual freedom, helped push anti-French sentiment into a political movement.

So great had Jahn's influence grown, that his students, then called Turners, caused the king to take notice. Jahn was imprisoned, and his school closed. The Turners then took to practicing at odd hours, where they could talk and work out without fear of being hassled by government officials. Jahn spent six years in prison.

During the 1800s, gymnastics competitions were held by various school, athletic, and ethnic

This fresco depicts the ancient sport of bull leaping. Using the bull's own strength as a springboard, gymnasts from the Minoan civilization on the island of Crete practiced vaulting in 2000 B.C.

In 1934, members of the French Society of Gymnasts form a giant pyramid with the help of a few ladders.

clubs such as the Turnvereins and Sokols, which were gymnastics schools in Europe. The sport still hadn't taken hold in America. At that time there was also much discussion among enthusiasts as to which form was the best and how to go forward.

By the 1860s, Jahn's form of gymnastics was being challenged by a new version created by Swedish gymnast Pehr Henrik Ling, who emphasized rhythm and coordination in routines played out with hoops and balls. That stood in stark contrast to Jahn's version, which pitted men against the apparatus.

German and Swedish natives emigrating to the United States brought their sport of gymnastics with them. But the sport didn't catch on much beyond those ethnic communities.

Immigrants Charles Beck, Charles Follen, and Francis Lieber are credited with introducing gymnastics into the U.S. school system during the 1830s. The program created for U.S. schools became a hybrid of the German and Swedish forms of gymnastics. The exercises did not immediately appeal to American school kids. Americans were used to games as a form of physical education rather than something requiring extensive practice of strenuous routines.

But the sport continued to gain popularity in Europe, where the Bureau of the European Gymnastics Federation, later renamed the International Gymnastics Federation (FIG), was formed in 1881 to set a path for international competition.

In the United States, the Amateur Athletic Union (AAU) was created in 1883 to regulate most amateur sports. Before then, clubs and local organizations around the country staged most gymnastics competitions.

The 1896 Olympics was the site of the first-ever large-scale gymnastics competition. Gymnasts from five countries participated in such events as the men's horizontal bar, parallel bars, pommel horse, rings, and vault. As expected, German gymnasts whipped the competition, walking off with the gold, silver, and bronze medals.

In 1903 in Antwerp, Belgium, the first international gymnastics competition was held

Mary Lou Retton, shown during her balance beam routine at the 1984 Olympics in Los Angeles, became the first American woman ever to win an individual Olympic gold medal in gymnastics.

outside of an Olympics. Gymnasts from four countries participated in what was then called the first World Championships. Some track and field events were also included in the tournament. The track events wouldn't fully disappear until 1954.

By 1904, men's gymnastics team competition was officially accepted into the Olympics at the St. Louis Games. But, because of the travel involved, 107 of the 119 gymnasts that competed were American.

During the 1920s, the FIG blended the German and Swedish forms of gymnastics in what was another step toward formalizing the sport. At the 1924 Olympics in Paris, men competed for individual Olympic medals on each apparatus and combined for a team medal.

Women's gymnastics made its debut at the 1928 Olympics with a team competition won by the Netherlands. The first American women's team competed in the 1936 Olympics in Berlin, Germany. But gymnastics still lacked much following or participation in the U.S.

Rhythmic gymnastics, where participants use a ball, a hoop, clubs, and a ribbon as they perform choreographed movements to music, was recognized by the International Gymnastics Federation in 1962, with the first official World Championships held in 1963. The U.S. sent its first rhythmic competitors to the World Championships in 1972; in 1984 the sport was sanctioned by the Olympics.

The United States Gymnastics Federation was formed in 1970 as the governing body of the sport in this country. The sport got its biggest boost in the United States during the Olympics held in the 1970s and early 1980s, when American television networks helped make heroes out of gymnasts from other countries by telling the stories of their lives away from the competition.

Among those gymnasts who captured the hearts of American viewers were a pigtailed girl named Olga Korbut from what was then the Union of Soviet Socialist Republics (USSR), who won three gold medals at the 1972 Olympics in Munich, and Nadia Comaneci, who won three gold medals at the 1976 Games in Montreal. Their heartfelt life stories, combined with magnificent performances in their competitions, made Korbut and Comaneci heroes to many young American gymnasts and television viewers who watched at home, glued to their sets, awaiting the judges' ruling on their performances.

Korbut and Comaneci inspired a young American girl named Mary Lou Retton to excel at the sport. Coached by Bela Karolyi, who had coached Comaneci to her gold medal performance, Retton went to the 1984 Olympics in Los Angeles. She won five medals, including the first-ever women's overall gold medal, bringing her instant fame, millions of fans, and her picture on boxes of Wheaties cereal. Retton in turn served as the inspiration for many of the gymnasts who would form the Olympic gold team of 1996.

ALL ABOUT
THE COMPETITION

3

Gymnastics have been part of the Olympics since the modern Games began in 1896 and have since become a staple of the summer Games. Every four years, the Games culminate in what has virtually been a lifelong obsession for most participants. Former American gymnastics star Mary Lou Retton was part of a local program when she was seven years old. All of the "Magnificent Seven" that took the gold medal at the 1996 Games started when they were young, too.

In Olympic competition, performances for artistic gymnastics are based on a 10-point system, rated by four to six specially trained judges. For each routine, a gymnast starts off with a less-than-perfect score. For men, that means a competitor starts with an 8.60 score; women start with a 9.00. Judges then make deductions for faults in the competitor's performance, either in execution, missed moves, or other requirements.

Judges can add bonus points—up to 1.40 for men and 1 point for women—which can bring the score up to a perfect 10.00.

Skills are divided into five levels of difficulty, ranging from easy to the most difficult. Under competition rules, each routine must have a minimum number of parts, which fluctuates depending on the level of competition.

Olympic gold medalist Dominique Moceanu performs a flip during her floor exercise at a gymnastics show held in Boston in 1997. After their success at the Olympics, the 1996 U.S. men's and women's teams toured the nation and performed in exhibitions.

Each judge comes up with a score for each competitor. The high and low scores are tossed out and the remaining figures are averaged to produce a competitor's score for an event.

The International Federation of Gymnastics, located in Moutier, Switzerland, sets standards for each of the competitions. Under the current guidelines, men compete in six different events and women compete in four events. Each event requires one compulsory routine—a series of moves designed to display exact skills as defined by the sanctioning organization—and one optional routine in which participants can string together a series of moves to display their athletic ability.

A gymnastics team consists of seven athletes, six of whom compete in each event, with the five highest scores going toward the overall team score.

Among the men's events are:

FLOOR EXERCISE

In this event, an athlete completes a series of movements performed without an apparatus on a mat 40' square. The whole floor area must be used during the routine, which usually consists of tumbling passes, at least one forward and backward roll, and some form of a balance move in which the athlete holds himself still on one leg or one arm. The routine lasts between 50 and 70 seconds. The entire routine must also be done with some sense of rhythm and harmony.

POMMEL HORSE

The pommel horse is considered the most difficult of all men's gymnastics routines. Athletes must complete a routine on a leather-covered apparatus, which has two covered handles in the middle that are between 15.7" and 17.7" apart. The typical routine consists of swinging and circling with the torso and legs, using only the hands for support. The difficulty comes because most of the moves are swirling motions on what is a straight pommel horse. Plus, most of the routine is done on one arm, as the athlete is continuously switching hands on each handle.

STILL RINGS

Using two rings suspended above the ground, an athlete completes a routine that combines still and rapid movements. Participants must include two handstands during their routines

Bart Conner demonstrates great strength and control on the still rings, which are supposed to remain as motionless as possible while the gymnast is performing.

and one element of strength that must be held for at least two seconds. One of the most difficult strength moves is the cross, where the athlete positions his body in either a straight or L-shape and then extends his arms perpendicular to his body. This is all done with unstable rings suspended by cables. The key to the event is executing moves with the least amount of movement in the rings or body.

VAULT

Participants run toward a horse—a leather-covered object much like the pommel horse, but without handles—then jump on a springboard that propels them into the air, where they place their hands on the horse, completing a series of acrobatic moves while airborne. The horse stands 4.4' high and is 5.2' long. Gymnasts must demonstrate a rise in the height of their body after pushing off the horse and travel at least eight feet. Then they must complete the routine with a solid landing, without extra steps.

PARALLEL BARS

Athletes must execute a series of moves while supporting themselves on two flexible wooden bars as much as 20.5" apart and 6.4' above the ground. Routines consist of a series of balancing, swinging, and airborne actions. Strength demonstrations may be part of the routine, though they are not required. Athletes are limited to no more than three stops or hold positions during a routine. Likewise, as part of the requirements, athletes must complete one release move, where both hands break contact with the bars.

Blaine Wilson performs on the parallel bars on his way to winning the all-around title at the U.S. Gymnastics Championships held in Sacramento, California, in August 1999. Wilson became the first person to win the title four times in a row.

HORIZONTAL BAR

Using a single bar suspended 9' above the ground, athletes complete a series of moves that require continuous swinging motions and frequent changes in direction. Most of the routine consists of giant swings of the participant's body, often requiring a change in the position of his grip or body. Like the parallel bars, a participant in the horizontal event must at one point release and grasp the bar again during his routine. The athlete usually

Mary Lou Retton vaults over the horse during the 1984 Olympics in Los Angeles, where she scored a perfect 10 for this event. The vault is basically the same in men's and women's competition, with height, distance, and the landing providing the basis for scoring.

ends his routine with a soaring dismount, often including a somersault or flip, before hitting the ground solidly on both feet.

WOMEN'S EVENTS

Among the women's competition, only two are done in a similar fashion to the men's competition: the vault and floor exercises.

VAULT

In the women's vault competition, the horse, while the same shape and size as the men's version, is lowered in height to 3.9" and is approached from the side. The very best in the vault competition soar off the springboard and get their feet over their heads rapidly before executing a twist or turn off the horse. Judges in the vault event look for height and distance traveled as well as a solid landing.

FLOOR EXERCISE

The women's floor event takes place on the same 40' square mat as the men's floor exercise. But the women's floor exercise lasts between 70 and 90 seconds—slightly longer than the men's event—and must be performed to music. A good routine on the floor includes moves that are blended together and one that includes high points, or specific acrobatic moves. Like the men's competition, the women must use the entire mat surface and change directions several times. Judges not only look for athletic ability but also some form of theatrics or showmanship.

Where the women's events differ most from the men's are in the uneven bars and balance beam routines.

UNEVEN BARS

The uneven bars require athletes to complete a routine of moves on two bars set at different heights. One bar is placed at 7.9' high, while the other is set at 5.2'. The routine, similar to the men's parallel bars activities, requires constant swinging, releasing, and changing directions. It's considered the most spectacular of the women's events because of the daring moves attempted by participants. The uneven bars require precision, split-second timing, complete focus, and strength. A good routine will have excellent flow from one move to the next with no pauses in action. Each routine must have two release moves, where the participant loses touch with the bars.

BALANCE BEAM

In the balance beam event, athletes complete their entire routines on a long beam, just 4" wide. Everything is done on a piece of wood about as wide as a sandwich that is 3.9' above the ground. Participants do a series of moves, such as rolls, cartwheels, handsprings, and jumps. The goal of the beam—which must include one acrobatic series with two jumping elements—is to make the entire routine look as if it took place on a mat, rather than on the beam.

RYTHMIC GYMNASTICS

Rythmic gymnastics combines dance and gymnastics. Recognized by the International Federation of Gymnastics in 1962, the first rythmic gymnastics competition was held at the World Championships in Budapest, Hungary, in 1963. The rules for rythmic gymnastics,

Russia's Alin Kabayera uses a rope during her performance in the women's rhythmic gymnastics finals at the 1998 Goodwill Games. Rhythmic gymnastics combines movement with music and equipment such as rope, ribbons, hoops, and balls. Routines must be executed in a graceful, flowing manner that keeps a rhythm.

while no less athletic, are dramatically different. The sport requires a high level of skill, strength, power, flexibility, and agility. There is no fixed apparatus used in rhythmic gymnastics. Instead, athletes perform their routines holding such objects as ribbons, hoops, balls, and clubs. Routines with each item include swings, throws, catches, tosses, spins, passes, and balancing. Gymnasts perform moves that demonstrate their coordination, including balancing acts, jumps, and pivots.

Each activity is performed to music. Participants are judged on composition, the difficulty of what she does, and the execution. The key is to execute a routine that easily blends the equipment in a graceful move. There are also team events during which five athletes perform together.

Each individual exercise is limited to 90 seconds with the group events lasting as long as two-and-a-half minutes. Rhythmic gymnasts must demonstrate the coordination and control of a dancer, as well as athletic ability. But while athletes can execute rolls or tumbles, no jumps or handsprings are allowed.

Scoring is similar to artistic gymnastics; competitors start out with a base score, and points are awarded or taken away based on the performance. There are two panels of judges for each routine, with one watching composition and the other judging execution.

Senior athletes start out with a base score of 19.40 points, with bonuses of .60 allowed for exceptional performances, up to a maximum score of 20.00 points. The base score of a group event is 19.20 points, with bonus points allowing for a possible 20.00 score.

4 WOMEN LEAD THE WAY

The sport of gymnastics owes a large portion of its popularity to women. Indeed, a sport created by men, and in the early years played exclusively by men, has become an international phenomenon because of the performances of several key women throughout history.

One of the first women to bring attention to gymnastics was Larissa Latynina, who during her career won 18 Olympic medals, nine of them gold, a record for any sport. Latynina was born in Kerhson, in the Soviet Socialist Republic of Ukraine, now known simply as the Ukraine. She attended the Kiev State Institute, where she trained as a ballerina and participated in gymnastics. By the time she was 16, Latynina was a national gymnastics champion.

Latynina excelled at the sport. At the 1956, 1960, and 1964 Olympic Games, she won the floor exercise events, and her team won the overall gold medals. Twice she won the all-around competition. Outside of the Olympics, Latynina won eight gold medals, four silver, and one bronze at the World Championships. When she retired from competition, Latynina went on to coach Soviet gymnastics teams.

Had Latynina participated in the sport during the 1970s, '80s, or '90s, she no doubt would have been a household name. But her time was before television grasped hold of the Olympics as

Tiny 14-year-old Nadia Comaneci enchanted audiences at the 1976 Olympic Games in Montreal, Canada, where she racked up seven perfect scores of 10—the first perfect scores ever granted in Olympic gymnastics competition.

a major broadcasting event, making each of the participants heroes.

Latynina earned more medals than Nadia Comaneci or Olga Korbut, whose names became familiar throughout the world. While Korbut has fewer medals, she may have done more than anyone to boost the sport's profile in the United States and around the world.

Korbut was born in 1956 in Grodno in the former Belorussian Soviet Socialist Republic, now the republic of Belarus. She wasn't a particularly strong student, though she caught the eye of a teacher who noticed her athletic ability during a physical education class. At the urging of the teacher, she entered a government sports school at age 11. At the school she was taken under the wing of Renald Knysh, who was known for pushing his students to feats previously not attained by other gymnasts.

Only 4' 10" tall, she stood out among her competitors. Despite her size, she was willing to attempt moves on the apparatus not tried in competition before by other athletes.

"My coach said I would never be a gymnast because I was different," Korbut told the *Austin American-Statesman* in 1999. "In 1962 and '64, gymnasts were tall, skinny, beautiful. When we start[ed] to do new gymnastics, I was punished by head coaches. They said we don't need this gymnastics. It's very hard gymnastics. I was from [a] small city first of all, not from Moscow, not from Minsk. They don't need me."

Korbut stuck it out and worked hard. As the '60s came to a close, Korbut was among the best Soviet gymnasts. She finished fifth in the 1969 National Championships and a year later was first in the vault competition at the USSR National Championships. Her performance gained her a spot as an alternate for the Soviet national team.

Like most Olympic athletes, Korbut set aside everything in her life for a shot at a gold medal. "When you have a goal, a dream, this will not be hard," she told *USA Today* in 1999. "Yes of course, you can't eat, smoke, or drink. You can't have a boyfriend, nothing. But you have a big goal and this is life. Gymnastics was in my heart."

Her sacrifices paid off, though. By 1972, Korbut was at the top of her game. She finished third all-around at the USSR National Championships. She was first at another international tournament, and she was named an alternate for the 1972 Olympic team. Then, when another gymnast was hurt before the Olympics, Korbut was elevated to full team status.

Korbut entered the 1972 summer Olympic competition in Munich, West Germany, as the second-best gymnast on her team. First ranked was Ludmilla Tourischeva, the world champion. In the first day of competition, Korbut proved to everyone that she was worthy of the first team. But by day two, she fell behind to seventh place overall. She left the parallel bars crying.

Still, her outgoing spirit, pigtails, and smile made her a magnet for the television cameras beaming the games out to a worldwide audience. More importantly, her petite size and earlier training gave her an edge others didn't have. She was daring.

Her determination paid off on the third day of competition when she displayed a loop in the uneven bars never seen before, as well as a never-before-completed head over heels backward somersault on the balance beam. The moves were immediately dubbed the "Korbut loop" and the "Korbut flip."

"I brought a lot of new elements," she said. "I did the back flip 100 times every day, 10 years before I show it to the public."

Korbut rebounded from her disastrous second day to earn gold medals in the balance beam and floor exercise and a silver medal in the uneven bars. She also picked up a gold for the overall team competition. In an Olympics that was expected to focus on American pixie Cathy Rigby, Korbut became a star.

Almost immediately—thanks to television announcers stressing her troubles—Americans and fans around the globe fell in love with Korbut. Her ear-to-ear smiles brought some light to an Olympic games that were otherwise marred by disaster. During the games, Palestinian guerrillas stormed the dorm rooms housing the Israeli Olympic team and killed 11 athletes. The resulting siege also resulted in the deaths of five terrorists and one police officer.

"I think I brought a new gymnastics to the world in all ways," Korbut told the *Los Angeles Times* in 1992. "I feel that at that time, gymnastics was not very interesting and I made it more interesting so more people would gravitate to it."

And people gravitated to Korbut. Overnight she became a worldwide celebrity. The government used her to promote the sport and the country. She has said that the hardest time in

her life was right after the 1972 Olympics. Her constantly busy schedule prohibited her from learning new routines and preparing for the 1976 Games.

"Everybody started to recognize me," she said. "Everybody talked about me. I wasn't ready for that. Wherever I went, they gave things to me for free."

The work she had to do for the Russian government hampered training. Before the 1972 Games she was dedicated to the sport; after the Olympics she spent a lot of time away from the gym.

"That's why I didn't want to compete in 1976 because I wasn't ready enough to show

Olga Korbut of the Soviet Union supports herself above the balance beam during her performance in the women's overall gymnastics program at the Montreal Olympics in 1976. Korbut scored a 9.5 for her routine.

[the] public. Not judges. Public. I loved [the] public very much," she said.

"I never competed for judges or medals," she added. "I competed to show how I can do better in gymnastics. From 1972 on I wasn't home. Right after the Olympic Games I was all over the world and it was very hard. I was empty inside. Empty emotionally. That was very important. If heart empty, you can't even smile."

Korbut did compete in the 1976 Olympics, but by then, the spotlight was on another relative newcomer, Nadia Comaneci. Born in 1961 in Onesti, Romania, Comaneci was noticed by Romanian gymnastics coach Bela Karolyi when she was six years old. He signed her up for the Romanian junior gymnastics team. In 1970, at age nine, she won the junior National Championship. She continued to dominate in contests among her age group, winning the all-around title and three individual events in the 1975 senior European Championships.

At age 14, she led the Romanian gymnastics contingent to Montreal, Canada, site of the 1976 Olympics. Comaneci felt she couldn't beat Korbut and simply hoped for a medal of any sort. She was wrong. Korbut's fears of not practicing enough were proven correct. She was exhausted. Comaneci won three gold medals, two silvers, and a bronze. She was the first gymnast to ever earn a perfect 10 score, achieving perfection seven times.

The first perfect score, which she earned for the uneven bars, came as a shock to Comaneci. "I finished my routine and I thought it was one of the best, and maybe I would get a 9.9," Comaneci recalled. "Then

I went back and started to prepare myself mentally for the beam routine. I wasn't looking for the score and I heard the crowd explode. I looked up at the board and I saw a 1.0, because the scoreboard didn't go to 10, and I didn't get why the crowd was so wild. But then I got it and I waved and smiled to the crowd. Bela [Karolyi, her coach] came over and hugged me, and then he said, 'Remember, you have to do the beam, so cut!'"

Like Korbut, Comaneci's life changed almost immediately. She, too, became an immediate television star in the United States and worldwide. When she returned home there were so many fans at the airport that she was afraid to get off the airplane.

"I kept looking for my mom in the crowd, because she did not go to the Olympics," she said. "And I remember I was carrying this doll that a fan had once given me. And I loved that doll. I held it tight, but in the crowd its leg got knocked off and it lost an arm, and I kept saying, 'Mom, mom, my doll . . .'

"I could not believe the attention," she added. "People would come and stand in front of my house just to visit it. It happened the entire year and it was overwhelming for me."

AMERICA BRINGS HOME THE GOLD

Nadia Comaneci's performance at the 1976 Olympics inspired millions of little girls around the world to take up gymnastics. For Mary Lou Retton, Comaneci inspired greatness.

Born in Fairmont, West Virginia, in 1968, Retton signed up for a gymnastics class for kids at West Virginia University when she was seven years old.

Within a few years she was considered one of the best in her class in the United States. By 1981 she was named to the U.S. junior national team. Retton garnered the attention of renowned coach Bela Karolyi, who had moved to the United States after coaching Comaneci to Olympic records.

Retton was invited to train at the U.S. Gymnastics Center in Houston, Texas, where Karolyi schooled his students. Retton moved to Texas, and a year later, under Karolyi's tutelage, she became the first American woman to win the all-around title at Japan's Chunichi Cup competition. She also won the first of what would become three consecutive American Cups.

Retton, a spunky, petite star with physical strength far beyond her size, attacked the gymnastics apparatus with vigor. Unlike her idols Nadia Comaneci and Olga Korbut, who were known for their long legs and balletic performances, Retton was compact, athletic, and muscular.

As a warm-up to the 1984 Olympics in Los Angeles, Retton appeared in the McDonald's

Sixteen-year-old Mary Lou Retton of the U.S. exults after performing a perfect 10 on the vault at the 1984 summer Olympics in Los Angeles. Retton also earned a perfect 10 for her floor exercise.

American Cup competition, held before a crowd of 12,377 at New York City's Madison Square Garden. Retton earned a 10 in the vault, a 9.95 in the uneven bars, a 9.80 on the balance beam, a 9.75 in floor exercise, and a 10 in the floor exercise on the second day.

"I thought I could have done a little better this time on the floor," Retton said afterward, "but I didn't have much pressure." For the second straight year, she and gymnast Peter Vidmar earned the all-around titles.

"She can provide the biggest surprise of any woman in the history of women's gymnastics, because she hasn't done that much in international competition," Karolyi said following the McDonald's American Cup tournament. "She is still a relative unknown internationally, and that should make it very exciting."

But Mary Lou Retton's path to the 1984 Olympics was almost sidetracked by a serious injury. Her knee had been hurting all year. But she figured it was an ordinary injury that would go away. It didn't, though.

Six weeks before the Games, she was resting after a workout. "I sat down Indian style at the end of the floor exercise mat and the little girls wanted some autographs, and 20, 25 minutes passed, and I went to stand up and I couldn't," Retton told the *Los Angeles Times*. "My knee was actually locked crooked. I hobbled up to Bela and tapped him on the hip and I said, 'Bela, I can't straighten my knee.' His eyes kind of crossed and he said, 'You're crazy.'"

Karolyi took Retton back to the hotel where she was staying and told her to put ice on it. The next day, Retton's knee was drastically swollen. A trip to the hospital emergency room revealed that she had cracked the cartilage in her knee. She was told she needed surgery. To any athlete, there are no scarier words than "you need surgery." In most cases, an extensive rehabilitation process follows surgery. Other times, the results mean an end to a career. All of those thoughts went through the minds of Retton and Karolyi.

Karolyi sent Retton to a top orthopedic surgeon, who suggested a then relatively new arthroscopic surgery, in which the surgery is performed through a small tube inserted into the knee. Mary Lou left training the next morning, had the surgery, and was back in training two days later. Outside of a few teammates and her parents, no one was told of the injury.

"We did three months of rehabilitation in two weeks," she said. "In gymnastics, we're vaulting, we're 10 and 11 feet up in the air, we're coming down on our legs. I mean, to get back into that kind of shape that fast is just unheard of. But I remember when the doctor gave me the release, saying, 'Let's land on it, let's see if this knee is going to hold up. It was a vault with a front handspring and . . . I landed it."

She entered the 1984 Olympics as a favorite in the gymnastics competition. The Games, held in Los Angeles, were boycotted by the Soviet Union in retaliation for the U.S. boycott of the 1980 Olympics in Moscow. As a result, some of the best competitors were not part of the games. But still part of the games, and considered the best of the bunch, were the Romanians.

The Americans didn't have the depth of the Romanians and finished second for the silver medal in team competition.

"It was just like I dreamed it, the excitement, the tension, the crowd, the feeling you have standing on the podium with an Olympic medal," Retton told *Time* magazine of the team medal. But she couldn't help but notice that the Romanian team's gold medals were shinier than the American team's silver ones.

The night before the final in the women's individual competition, Retton lay in bed and as she had so many other times before, imagined herself going through the motions of her routines—perfectly. She would have to do it without her coach lending support. Karolyi had been barred from the actual competition by Don Peters, the U.S. coach, who didn't want Karolyi around. But Karolyi gained access to the competition floor by landing a job as an equipment adjuster. Before each event Retton would scan the crowd for Karolyi.

If her knee was troubling Retton, it wasn't showing on the competition floor.

At the start of the all-around contest, Retton led the field. Hot on her tail was Romania's top gymnast, Ecaterina or "Kati" Szabo. In the beam competition, Szabo earned a perfect 10 score. Retton then earned a 9.5 on the uneven bars, which tied the score. In the second series, Retton earned a 9.80 on the balance beam. Szabo then scored a 9.95 on the floor exercise, giving her a .15 lead over Retton.

Retton was next up on the floor exercise, a routine at which she excelled. On her first run, Retton hit a layout double somersault, which set the tone for the rest of the routine. When she landed, she had earned a 10 score. Szabo rebounded, earning 9.90s on the vault and the uneven bars.

Romania's Ecaterina Szabo was Mary Lou Retton's biggest competition at the 1984 Olympics. Szabo won gold medals in the floor exercise and the side horse but finished second to Retton in the all-around competition.

As Retton stood waiting for her turn on the vault, Karolyi reached across a photographer's barricade and showed Retton a slip of paper, where he had calculated the scores. She needed a 9.95 to tie Szabo; a 10 would give her the all-around title. The vault was Retton's best event. On her way to the apparatus, Retton stepped in a small puddle of a soft drink.

"That's all right," Peters told her. "It will help you stick when you land on your vault."

The green light flashed, indicating Retton could make her first attempt at the exercise. Karolyi had told her to go flat onto the horse, which would provide her with more height. She knew in the air, as she performed her twist called a Tsukahara, that she had hit the vault perfectly.

"And when I landed, the noise went up and Bela jumped over the fence and Pauley Pavilion [site of the Los Angeles gymnastics competition] was going nuts," Retton recalled. "And it seemed like an hour before they flashed the score of a 10, and yeah, I had stuck it. I had scored 10's on my vault many times in other competitions. So I knew I was capable of doing it. But they still had to flash the score. And it seemed like an eternity."

With the perfect 10, Retton was already the gold medal winner. However, she still had an opportunity to do the event again if she so desired. She did, and she earned another perfect 10 on her second attempt.

"That was more prestigious to me, the second vault, than even the first," Karolyi said. "Usually the second vault is a better vault. . . . But, prior to this performance, I never in 35 years [have] seen one gymnast [who] managed to do a second perfect vault after a perfect vault, or the vault which made her a winner."

That night, Retton slept with her gold medal under her pillow. "The first thing when I got up in the morning I checked to see if it wasn't a dream." Retton was the first American woman to capture the all-around Olympic gold medal.

In addition to her gold medal for the women's all-around competition and her silver women's team medal, Retton won a silver in the vault competition and two bronze medals—one for the uneven bars and one for the floor exercise. With five 1984 Olympic medals, Retton is tied for the most medals ever won by an American woman. As with Olga Korbut and Nadia Comaneci before her, Retton was turned into an international celebrity immediately.

Retton wasn't alone in taking home the gold at the 1984 Olympics. Bart Conner won two gold medals at the Games.

Born in Chicago, Conner started participating in gymnastics when he was just 10 years old. Soon he was successful in junior competition and was part of the Olympic team that competed in Montreal in 1976. He didn't win a medal there.

Conner won several competitions between 1976 and 1983, although during the '83 season he suffered a severe muscle tear in his arm. The injury prevented him from competing in the 1984 U.S. National Championships, which is part of the qualifying process for the Olympic team.

He was allowed to compete in the Olympic trials, where his performance was strong enough to earn a place on the team. In the Olympics he won a gold medal on the parallel bars and helped lead the U.S. to a team gold medal. He retired after the Olympics and in 1996 married Nadia Comaneci.

At the 1984 Games, Peter Vidmar generated the highest total ever for an American man in the all-around competition. The Los Angeles

Peter Vidmar, captain of the men's gymnastics team at the 1984 Olympics, tied for first place on the pommel horse.

native began gymnastics at an early age and excelled at the sport while attending the University of California at Los Angeles (UCLA). He won the U.S. National all-around title in 1980 and 1982 and the National Collegiate Athletic Association's all-around title in 1983 and 1984.

Going into the 1984 Olympics, Vidmar was named captain of the men's team. There, he

Bart Conner, of the U.S., performs on the parallel bars during the 1984 summer Olympics. Conner won a gold medal for this performance.

won a gold medal, the first Olympic medal won by the U.S. in team competition since 1932. He tied for first place in the pommel horse and second in the all-around competition. He retired from the sport after the Games.

Despite the magnificent feats by Conner and Vidmar at the 1984 Games, Retton's broad smile and perky attitude overshadowed their efforts. Americans and the media fell in love with the gymnast. Her smiling picture was featured on a box of Wheaties cereal, a spot reserved for the world's best athletes. She was in demand for promotional and commercial jobs and averaged 50 speaking appearances a year.

In 1984 the Associated Press named her amateur athlete of the year, and *Sports Illustrated* honored her as "Sportswoman of the Year." In 1985 she was inducted into the U.S. Olympic Hall of Fame. Retton's fame was not fleeting. In 1993, nearly a decade after her gold medal victory in Los Angeles, she was voted "Most Popular Athlete in America" by an Associated Press survey. In 1995 she was awarded the Flo Hyman Award from the Women's Sports Foundation for her accomplishments both in competition and away from the sport. Retton was inducted into the International Gymnastics Hall of Fame in 1997.

Though she retired from competition in 1986, Retton has done more to promote the sport of gymnastics than anyone else. She's a regular on the speech circuit, giving motivational talks based on her Olympic experience, and she has written a motivational book called *Gateways to Happiness*. She has served as an inspiration for the young gymnasts who took up the sport after her magical performance at the 1984 summer Olympics in Los Angeles.

Retton's gold medal performance was a long way from the ones won by Larissa Latynina so many years ago. The sport had changed dramatically in that time, something Latynina noticed herself.

"The gymnastics of our time was very different from today's sport with its amazingly difficult elements and combinations," Latynina, a 1956 gold medal winner, told the Russian Information Agency, TASS, in 1987.

"Today's girls grow more tired in two or three years than we did in ten, and I mean not so much physical as psychological fatigue. A fast-moving pace is a sign of life, not only sport, today."

6 THE CURRENT AND FUTURE STARS

In 1963, when USA Gymnastics was founded as the sole national governing body for gymnastics in the United States, there were just 7,000 athletes competing on a limited schedule.

At the time, the only major international events for gymnastics were the Olympics and the Pan American Games.

Today there are 71,000 participants registered in competitive gymnastics programs with more than 13,000 people registered as professionals and instructors.

More than 3,000 sanctioned contests and events are held annually throughout the U.S. alone. The staff of USA Gymnastics has grown from three to 40 people.

Outstanding young gymnasts among men include Blaine Wilson, John Roethlisberger, Yewki Tomita, Sean Townsend, and Chris Young. On the women's side, some of the hopefuls are Kristen Maloney, Vanessa Atler, Jennie Thompson, Alyssa Beckerman, and Jamie Dantzscher.

Born in 1974 and raised in Ohio, Blaine Wilson was a national champion each year from 1996 to 1999 and a bronze medallist in the 1998 Goodwill Games. He began in gymnastics in 1979 and has been a member of the senior National team since 1993.

John Roethlisberger is a two-time Olympian (1992, 1996) and is the son of an Olympian.

Vanessa Atler of Canyon Country, California, vaults the horse during the women's team finals at the 1999 World Gymnastics Championships. Atler began training as a gymnast when she was just five years old.

A Falcon Heights, Minnesota, native, Roethlisberger has been participating in gymnastics since 1978. He was named to the national team in 1989, was the 1990 national all-around champion, and has been a member of every major National team since.

Yewki Tomita is relatively new to the national team, having become a member of the senior squad in 1998. A native of Tucson, Arizona, Tomita began in gymnastics in 1986. His father, Yoichi, was also a National team member from 1979 to 1980. Yewki was a member of the U.S. team for the 1998 Goodwill Games, where he earned a bronze medal, and the 1999 World Championship team. He's known for his excellent bodylines and technical performance. He cites the still rings and vault as his favorite events.

Like Tomita, Sean Townsend has been part of the National team since 1998. A native of Texas, Townsend calls Dallas home. He started in the sport in 1988 and became a member of the junior National team in 1995. He cites the high bar as his favorite event, though he is known for big vaults.

Chris Young joined the national team in 1998. Born in Winston-Salem, North Carolina, Young took up the sport in 1983. His favorite event is the high bar, and he's known for his dynamic performances.

Among women's gymnastics hopefuls, Kristen Maloney is leading the way. The New Jersey native has been on the National team since 1993 and was the 1998 and 1999 national champion. She took the gold medal at the 1998 Goodwill Games and was part of the 1997 World Championships team. Maloney

took up gymnastics in 1987 and has said the floor exercise is her favorite event.

Vanessa Atler has been on the National team since 1994. A California native, she began gymnastics training in 1987 when she was just five years old.

The 1996 junior National champion and 1997 senior National cochampion, she was a member of the 1999 World Championships team and a double gold medal winner at the Goodwill Games in 1998.

Jennie Thompson, part of the National team since 1992, began training in gymnastics in 1986. Born in Texas, Thompson was the 1993 junior national champion and a member

Known for his form, Yewki Tomita of Tucson, Arizona, balances on the rings during the men's all-around individual competitions at the World Gymnastics Championships held in Tianjin, China, in 1999.

Jennie Thompson goes through her routine on the uneven bars during the final night of competition at the 1999 U.S. Gymnastics Championships. Thompson scored a 9.675 on the bars and tied with Jamie Dantzscher for the gold medal.

of the 1997 and 1999 World Championships team.

Alyssa Beckerman was born in Long Branch, New Jersey, and now resides in Wyoming, Ohio. She started in the sport in 1986 and cites the uneven bars as her favorite event. She joined the National team in 1997 and was a member of the 1999 World Championships team, the 1999 Pan American Games squad, and the 1999 Pontiac International Team Championships. She has accepted a gymnastics scholarship to UCLA, but she has deferred her enrollment until after the 2000 Olympics.

Jamie Dantzscher, a California native who took up gymnastics in 1989, was a member of the 1999 Pan American Games team, the '99 China Dual, and the '99 Pontiac International and World Championships teams.

While a "name" gymnast, someone recognized by people outside of gymnastics, has yet to emerge out of the current crop of athletes, one has to remember that before the 1972 Olympics few beyond the gymnastics community knew of a petite girl named Olga Korbut. And they didn't know about Mary Lou Retton before the 1984 Games. But a spectacular performance before a worldwide television audience can turn any one of the current team members into an overnight sensation.

Famous or not, the athletes now participating in the sport are similar to those at the start of the sport. They are fine-tuned individuals attempting to put together a perfect routine on an apparatus. The main difference, though, is that today if a gymnast earns a perfect score, he or she is likely to end up on a box of Wheaties.

CHRONOLOGY

2000 B.C.	Men and women of the Minoan culture participate in bull leaping, an early form of gymnastics.
100-400 A.D.	Gymnastics is taught in Greece as a way to condition military members, school children, and athletes.
1800s	Friendrich Ludwig Jahn creates a group of exercises using stationary apparatus to teach students self-discipline and strength.
1830s	Gymnastics programs begin in American schools.
1860s	Swedish gymnast Pehr Henrik Ling creates a new form of gymnastics emphasizing rhythm and coordination.
1881	The Bureau of European Gymnastics Federation, later renamed the International Gymnastics Federation, is formed to oversee international competition.
1883	The Amateur Athletic Union is created to oversee amateur sports in the United States.
1896	The first large-scale international gymnastics competition is held at the Olympics.
1903	In Antwerp, Belgium, the first large-scale non-Olympic gymnastic competition is held.
1904	Men's team gymnastics is accepted into Olympic competition.
1928	Women's team gymnastics becomes an Olympic event.
1962	Rhythmic gymnastics is recognized by the International Gymnastics Federation.
1970	The United States Gymnastics Federation is formed.
1972	Olga Korbut wins three gold medals in Munich and captures the eyes of the world.
1976	Nadia Comaneci becomes the first woman gymnast to earn a perfect 10 score.
1984	Mary Lou Retton wins five medals at the Los Angeles Olympics.
1996	The U.S. Women's gymnastics team captures the gold medal for all-around competition.

GLOSSARY

Aerial
A move during which the gymnast turns over in the air without touching the apparatus.

Apparatus
Pieces of equipment used by gymnasts to complete routines during a competition.

Compulsories
Routines that include specific movements required of all gymnasts.

Dismount
A move at the end of a routine in which the gymnast leaves an apparatus.

Execution
The performance of a gymnastics routine.

Giant
A move during which a gymnast's body is fully extended and swings 360 degrees around a bar.

Handspring
A move in which a gymnast springs off the hands by putting weight on the arms and pushing from the shoulders.

Optionals
Personally designed routines to show a gymnast's versatility and skills.

Release
A move during which a gymnast's hands are released from either parallel bar before regrasping it.

Routine
A combination of skills displayed on an apparatus or in a floor exercise.

FURTHER READING

Bolt, Jenny. *Rhythmic Gymnastics: The Skills of the Game*. Ramsey, Marlborough, England: The Crowwood Press, 1989.

Cohen, Joel. *Superstars of Women's Gymnastics*. Philadelphia: Chelsea House Publishers, 1998.

Dolan, Edward. *The Complete Beginner's Guide to Gymnastics*. New York: Doubleday & Co, 1980.

Feeney, Rik. *Gymnastics: A Guide for Parents and Athletes*. Lincolnwood, Illinois: Masters Press, 1995.

Rutledge, Rachel. *The Best of the Best in Gymnastics*. Brookfield, Connecticut: Millbrook Press, 1999.

Thomas, Kurt, and Kent Hannon. *Kurt Thomas on Gymnastics*. New York: Fireside Books, 1980.

WEBSITE

www.usa-gymnastics.org

INDEX

Amateur Athletic Union, 19

Atler, Vanessa, 53, 55

Beck, Charles, 19

Beckerman, Alyssa, 53, 56–57

Borden, Amy, 7

Bull leaping, 15

Chow, Amy, 7

Comaneci, Nadia, 10, 21, 34, 38–39, 41, 47

Conner, Bart, 47, 49

Dantzscher, Jamie, 53, 57

Dawes, Dominique, 7, 9

Follen, Charles, 19

Gymnastics
  history, 15–21
  men's events, 20, 24–28
  rules, 8–9, 23–24, 31
  women's events, 20, 28–31

International Gymnastics Federation, 19, 20, 24, 29

Jahn, Friendrich Ludwig, 16–18

Karolyi, Bela, 10–11, 12, 13, 21, 38, 39, 41, 42–43, 44, 45, 46

Knysh, Renald, 34

Korbut, Olga, 7, 21, 34–38, 39, 41, 47, 57

Latynina, Larissa, 33–34, 50–51

Lieber, Francis, 19

Ling, Pehr Henrik, 18

Maloney, Kristen, 53, 54–55

Miller, Shannon, 7, 9

Moceanu, Dominique, 7, 9, 10

Olympic Games, 7–13, 19, 20–21, 23, 33–34, 35–36, 37–39, 41, 42, 43–50, 53, 57

Peters, Don, 44, 46

Phelps, Jaycie, 7, 9

Retton, Mary Lou, 11, 13, 21, 23, 41–47, 49–50, 57

Rhythmic gymnastics, 20, 29–31

Rigby, Cathy, 36

Roethlisberger, John, 53–54

Sokols, 18

Strug, Kerri, 7, 9, 10–13

Szabo, Ecaterina, 44, 45

Thompson, Jennie, 53, 55–56

Tomita, Yewki, 53, 54

Townsend, Sean, 53, 54

Turners, 17

Turnvereins, 17, 18

USA Gymnastics, 53

Vidmar, Peter, 42, 47–49

Wilson, Blaine, 53

Young, Chris, 53, 54

PICTURE CREDITS Associated Press/WWP: pp. 2, 6, 8, 11, 20, 22, 25, 27, 28, 30, 37, 40, 45, 48, 49, 52, 55, 56, 58, 60; Corbis-Bettmann: pp. 17, 32; National Archives: p. 18; New York Public Library: p. 14.

RICHARD HUFF is an award-winning journalist. His previous books include *Behind The Wall: A Season on the NASCAR Circuit*, *The Insider's Guide to Stock Car Racing*, *The Making of a Race Car*, *The Jarretts*, *Demolition Derby*, and *Formula One Racing*. His work has appeared in such national publications as *Stock Car Racing* magazine, *Inside NASCAR*, *Seventeen*, *Video Review*, and *Circle Track*. He lives in New Jersey with his wife, Michelle, son Ryan, and daughter Paige.

ACKNOWLEDGMENTS Thanks to Michelle, Ryan, and Paige Huff.